CRIME SOLVERS

Hunting the cyber Trail

BE A COMPUTER FORENSIC SCIENTIST

by Alix Wood

Gareth Stevens
PUBLISHING

Please visit our website, **www.garethstevens.com**. For a free color catalog of
all our high-quality books, call toll free 1-800-542-2595 or fax 1-877-542-2596

Cataloging-in-Publication Data

Names: Wood, Alix.
Title: Hunting the cyber trail: be a computer forensic scientist / Alix Wood.
Description: New York : Gareth Stevens Publishing, 2018. | Series: Crime solvers | Includes index.
Identifiers: ISBN 9781538206379 (pbk.) | ISBN 9781538206317 (library bound) | ISBN 9781538206195
   (6 pack)
Subjects: LCSH: Computer crimes--Juvenile literature. | Computer crimes--Investigation--
   Juvenile literature. | Forensic sciences--Juvenile literature.
Classification: LCC HV8079.C65W66 2018 | DDC 363.25'968--dc23

First Edition

Published in 2018 by
Gareth Stevens Publishing
111 East 14th Street, Suite 349
New York, NY 10003

Copyright © 2018 Alix Wood Books

Produced for Gareth Stevens by Alix Wood Books
Designed by Alix Wood
Editor: Eloise Macgregor
Consultant: Stacey Deville, MFS, Texas Forensic Investigative
Consultants

Photo credits:
Cover, 1, 4, 5, 7 bottom, 8, 9, 10, 11, 13, 14, 15, 17, 20-21 background, 22, 27, 29, 30, 31, 32, 33, 35, 36, 38, 39,
40-41 background, 43 bottom © Adobe Stock Images, 6, 7 top, 43 top iStock, 12, 18, 20, 21, 25, 42 © Alix Wood,
26 © Timothy Harrison, 34 © Shutterstock, 41 inset © defense.gov, all other images are in the public domain

Printed in the United States of America
CPSIA compliance information: Batch #CS17GS For further information contact Gareth Stevens, New York, New York at 1-800-542-2595.

CONTENTS

Jethro Neale Goes Missing...

It's a beautiful summer evening. Jethro Neale tells his family he'll be back before dark, and heads out the door with his skateboard under his arm. He often goes out for a quick after-dinner skate before sunset.

His mom can see the skate park from the kitchen window. She sees the outline of her son land a kickflip as she and his sister, Kara, finish cleaning up. But Jethro doesn't come home before dark...

DISPATCHER: Emergency 911. What is the location of your emergency?

MOM: Hi, I'm from Walters Valley. I think my son has gone missing.

DISPATCHER: What is your name?

MOM: Agatha Neale.

DISPATCHER: How old is your son?

MOM: He's twelve.

DISPATCHER: What makes you think he is missing?

MOM: He didn't come back when he said he would. I've called all his friends...

Police Officer Peterson comes to speak to the family. He asks for the names and addresses of all Jethro's friends. He explains that people will sometimes tell more information to a police officer.

He asks if Jethro has any problems at home or school, or if he has made any new friends recently. Kara remembers that Jethro said he'd been talking to a new friend on a skate **chat room**.

Where's Jethro?

Officer Peterson thinks Jethro might come home by himself. If he doesn't, the next step will be to get a **computer forensic scientist** to collect his computer and look at his chat room history for clues.

Kara asks if she should check his computer, but Peterson says no. It is best if the experts look at the computer, in case anything she does spoils any **evidence**. Peterson asks them to call the police again if Jethro hasn't come home in a few hours. Peterson begins by checking Jethro's friends' houses. In many cases, a missing preteen is found asleep on a friend's sofa!

Solve It!

If you were Officer Peterson, what would you ask the family to give you?

a) a cup of coffee, it's going to be a long night

b) a recent photograph of Jethro

c) a map of the area in case you get lost

Answers on page 45

Date: July 21, 2017

Unit Number: 423

Reporting Officer's Notes

Reported missing: A 911 call was received at 10:55 p.m. from Agatha Neale, reporting her son as a missing person.

Last known whereabouts: Last seen at the Walters Valley skate park at around 7:30 p.m.

Description: White, 5 feet 4 inches (1.5 m) tall, medium-length curly red hair, wearing a green beanie hat, gray hoodie, blue jeans, and black and gray skate shoes. He was carrying a skateboard.

Witness statement: Jethro's sister Kara said Jethro had made a friend in a skate chat room and told her he was going to meet him.

Missing: Jethro Neale
Age: 12 years, two months
Address: 206 Valley Road, Walters Valley

A few hours later, Agatha Neale calls the police to say that Jethro has still not come home. The family is really worried now. Detective Olivier arranges to come over to the house. She'll bring a computer forensic specialist with her.

meet a computer forensic scientist

S cott Freeman has always loved tinkering with computers and solving problems. Being a computer forensic scientist means he not only solves computer problems — he also helps to solve crimes.

Whenever Scott collects a computer, he is always nervous that someone has tried to use it before he could look at it. Even something simple like switching the computer off can lose important information that he will never get back. He is pleased to see that Jethro's family has left the boy's computer exactly as it was. That will make his job much easier.

8

Name: Scott Freeman

Job: Computer Forensic Scientist

Education: Studied for a degree in computer science. Then studied for a certificate in computer forensics, followed by on-the-job training in the police department.

Career:
Scott started work at the police department as a trainee **technician**. He is now fully qualified.

Favorite school subject: Math

Favorite part of his job: You have to not only understand how computers work but also understand how a criminal may behave. It's challenging.

Worst part of his job: Sometimes I have to work very long hours.

Most interesting case: Scott investigated a case where a man was suspected of stealing from the company he worked for. Scott managed to trace all of the deleted **data** that helped track the missing money, proving the man's innocence. This information also led to the person who had deleted the data. This person ended up being the real thief.

Could You Crack a Code?

Sometimes computer forensic scientists have to find hidden data on computers. It is a little like cracking a code. How good would you be at code breaking? Try decoding the message below.

J335   J3   Q5   5YD   WIZ53   OQ41

Maybe you need a clue? Detectives found this instruction on a note hidden under the keyboard. Could it hold the key to unlocking the code?

Look up, and a little left.

Answers on page 45

Top Tip

Codes often follow a pattern. Once you have worked out the rule, it's easy to work out the message.

A criminal has sent a coded email to his **accomplice**. The computer forensic scientists think they have just had a breakthrough! There's a clue in the date the email was sent...the fourth! Can you work out what the coded message might say? The first word has been written in bold for you.

June 4 2017

Fred Badguy

To: Harvey Robber

Re: the 4th

Mr. Sanders and **I** have to see Will tomorrow. We shall meet Sam Harris and you must come too. At the moment all the crowd from Cathy's Corner will be there. Of course I might 1st go to the Street Café which is at bus stop number 10. Around about 4 p.m.?

Answers on page 45

COLLECTING THE EVIDENCE

Scott starts to pack up Jethro's computer. As it is still switched on, any information stored in the computer's **RAM** will still be there. RAM stands for Random Access Memory, and it stores any active information, which disappears when the computer is switched off. Scott's happy — he should be able to find yesterday's chat sessions.

Scott saves the RAM data quickly to disk. He looks around Jethro's bedroom for anything else that he should take back to his office.

Solve It!

Which of these items in Jethro's bedroom should Scott take with him to investigate?

a) the backpack

b) the computer **hard drive**

c) the snowboard

Answers on page 45

Computer evidence needs to be packed up carefully. Scott places everything into either paper bags, paper envelopes, or cardboard boxes. Plastic should never be used to store computer evidence, as it can produce **static electricity**. Plastic bags can also trap any moisture in the air, which may damage the evidence, too.

#26582

EVIDENCE BAG CHALLENGE

What is static electricity and why can it harm computers? Try this.

You will need: an empty soda can, a balloon

- Put the can on its side on a flat, smooth surface.

- Rub the balloon fast several times over your hair. This may make your hair stand on end!

- Hold the balloon so it is nearly touching the can. The can should start to roll toward the balloon.

Rubbing the balloon creates static electricity. **Electrons** created on the surface of the balloon will pull light objects toward them. In the same way, a plastic bag may damage delicate computer equipment.

Spaghetti Wires!

A big part of Scott's job when he collects a computer is to make sure that he remembers what was plugged in to what. He needs to put everything back how it was at Jethro's house to give him the best chance of tracking what Jethro last did online. Also, when a case goes to trial, the **defense** lawyer will try to make everything Scott says sound unreliable. Scott has to record everything exactly.

Top Tip

As wires are usually gray, Scott labels each wire with a letter. He then writes the correct letter on a sticker, and sticks it by the socket that wire came out of. He usually photographs the setup too.

14

Get a pen and paper. Write down which colored wire connects to which piece of equipment in the picture below. Test whether your system works by covering the picture and answering the quiz below using just your notes.

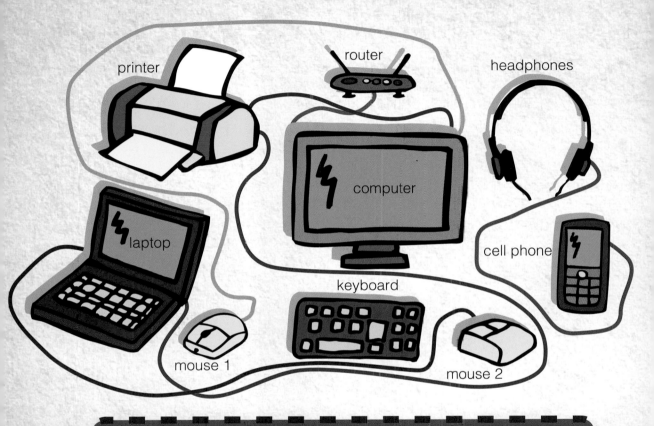

Solve It!

Cover up the picture above. Then try to answer these questions by looking at your notes. Don't peek!

1. What color wire connected the printer to the laptop?

2. What were the headphones connected to?

3. What two things did the yellow wire connect?

4. Was the computer connected to mouse 1 or mouse 2?

5. Which piece of equipment wasn't connected to anything else?

Answers on page 45

MOVING EVIDENCE

You would think that transporting evidence back to the office would be a very simple task. Load it in the trunk and off you go! When you are a computer forensic scientist, there are some important things that you need to do to keep the data and equipment in a useful state. Once Scott has placed everything in suitable containers, he needs to label everything correctly. A tiny mistake may mean that the device cannot be used as evidence in court.

Transport

How to Transport Digital Evidence

• Keep all digital evidence away from anything that may contain a magnet.	In a police car, radio **transmitters**, magnets in speakers, and magnetic mount emergency lights can all be a problem. Strong magnets can erase disks and create static electricity which can also harm the data.
• Don't keep digital equipment in the car for long.	Heat, cold, or **humidity** can all damage digital evidence.
• Package all devices well and keep them secured in the vehicle.	Digital devices can get damaged by **vibrations** and shocks.

If a device is powered by a battery, evidence such as dates, times, and settings may be lost in storage if the batteries fail. Scott must remember to tell the people who store the evidence if any devices are battery-powered. They will need to be examined quickly, before the battery goes dead.

Top Tip

Remember to collect all the power supplies and adapters for all the electronic devices that are seized, too.

Solve It!

What do you think Scott might use a "mouse-jiggler" for?

a) a mouse-jiggler is a special breed of mouse that can understand computer code.

b) a mouse-jiggler is a tool that shows how big a hand the last person who used the mouse had.

c) a mouse-jiggler is a device that keeps the computer from going to sleep by automatically jiggling the mouse.

Answers on page 45

copy everything!

Scott copies the RAM files, and then makes a copy of everything else on the computer. Computer forensic scientists always work using a copy of the original files. They never work on the actual device. This is because everything you do on a computer can make tiny changes to the data. They want the original computer to stay just as it was.

Top Tip

Special programs check that the copied data is identical to the original. The original computer is then stored securely.

Scott looks at Jethro's "Recent Items." There is plenty of information that will interest Detective Olivier. Jethro may have sent or received an email that could help explain where he was. His SkateGame Pro chat room conversations may show he was planning on meeting someone at the skate park. There may even be a clue in Jethro's English homework, or skate park photos.

Recent Items

Force Quit

Sleep

Applications
@ Email
Internet Browser
SkateGame Pro
Calendar

Documents
My Addresses
English Homework
Skate park Photos
Geography Essay

Servers

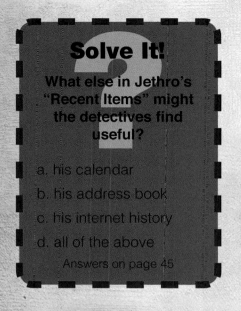

Solve It!

What else in Jethro's "Recent Items" might the detectives find useful?

a. his calendar

b. his address book

c. his internet history

d. all of the above

Answers on page 45

Scott starts to collect information to pass on to Detective Olivier. He carefully logs everything that he does. Computer forensic scientists must record exactly what they do on a device. Anyone should be able to read their log, follow the instructions, and get the same results. This means that other people can double-check that everything Scott says he has found is really there.

EVIDENCE BAG CHALLENGE

Imagine you went missing from school. Would one of your friends be able to help the detectives? Could they recall what you were wearing? If you were carrying a bag? What your hair was looking like? What color your eyes are? Test a friend and see how well they do.

You will need: a pen and paper, a friend

1. Write down a list of questions about your appearance, like the questions above.

2. Tell your friend that you are going to leave some questions on a table for them to answer. Don't tell them what the questions are about.

3. Leave the room for ten minutes, then go back and see how well your friend did!

SCIENCE DETECTIVE

Chat Room Friends

Scott finds Jethro's last chat room conversation. Jethro talked to three friends in the chat room on the day he disappeared.

skateboard chat

Hi. Which cheap skateboard trucks are the best? Any ideas?

Jethro03 11:05 a.m.

Hi Jethro03. I have some great ones I've hardly used. I am selling them cheap. Want to meet somewhere?

DanDares2 11:08 a.m.

Hey Jethro. I just got some new ones. I'll show you them tonight if you're at the park.

DavidD04 11:15 a.m.

Thanks guys. See you at Walters Valley later.

Jethro03 11:35 a.m.

Hi Jethro! You going around 7? Show me how to do a kickflip again!

DebbieSkates 11:43 a.m.

Jethro talked about meeting all three chat room friends that day. His sister said he was going to meet a new friend. Look at the clues in the chat messages and their **profiles** and see if you can work out who that was.

USERNAME: DanDares2

PROFILE: Joined the chat room a month ago. His profile says he is 14 years old and lives near Walters Valley.

USERNAME: DavidD04

PROFILE: Joined the chat room a year ago, the same day as Jethro did. His profile says he is 12 years old and lives in Walters Valley.

USERNAME: DebbieSkates

PROFILE: Joined the chat room two months ago. Her profile says she is 13 years old and goes to school at Walters Valley.

Solve It!

Which of the three people do you think Jethro hadn't met before?

a) DanDares2

b) DavidD04

c) DebbieSkates

Answers on page 45

21

Examining Photographs

Jethro has now been missing for two days. Everyone is worried. Scott has a look through the photographs on Jethro's computer. Detective Olivier has asked Scott to concentrate on finding any images of the skate park. He looks in the folder and finds quite a few, but none are very recent.

Scott wonders if Jethro may have thrown some images in the computer's trash. Using a special program, Scott can still find files even if they have been deleted. The images won't look like pictures anymore, they will just be streams of letters and numbers.

Top Tip

Computers are great detective tools in the right hands. Virtually everything done on a computer can be found by a computer forensics expert.

EVIDENCE BAG CHALLENGE

Scott can piece the images together again if he can find the section of code. But how does he find the right section in a stream of code like the one below? Different types of data have particular sets of numbers and letters at the start and end of their code. Scott has to search through to find those magic numbers.

Most images are saved as **JPEG** files. JPEGs begin with the code FF D8, and end with FF D9. Can you find the two JPEGs in the code below? It's not that easy!

```
2D 2C 2C 00 01 24 1F FF 2F 34 29 2A 34 35 0E 17
1C FF 24 2C FF D8 FF E0 10 10 4A 46 49 46 00 01
01 00 00 01 14 13 12 15 12 10 12 14 14 16 12 17
12 15 15 14 18 18 14 15 15 14 19 1C 26 1C 1E 17
EA 6A 32 FF 00 4F 76 7E F2 CB D8 DF 88 FF D9 50
4B 03 04 14 00 06 00 FF 00 00 00 21 00 96 B5 AD
E2 96 FF D8 FF E0 AD 6B FE 23 6B EF D2 75 D8 83
37 2A B4 FB 11 D6 B7 C9 3F E6 7A 8E c$ 27 3A AD
E8 00 96 58 83 05 79 3B 13 FF D9 80 01 C3 BA 61
```

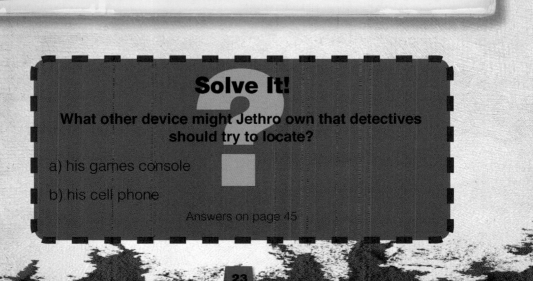

Solve It!

What other device might Jethro own that detectives should try to locate?

a) his games console

b) his cell phone

Answers on page 45

Decode Hexadecimal

Some programmers use a special code called hexadecimal. We usually count using ten digits, 0 through 9, probably because we have ten fingers! If we had sixteen fingers, we might count in base sixteen instead, known as hexadecimal. For the sixteen digits, programmers use 0 through 9, and add six letters, A, B, C, D, E, and F.

This chart shows how the alphabet is written in hexadecimal. The code for each letter is made up of the row number (down the left-hand side), followed by the column number or letter (running along the top). To decode the message on page 25 you won't need the top couple of rows.

	0	1	2	3	4	5	6	7	8	9	A	B	C	D	E	F
0																
1																
2	space	!	"	#	$	%	&	'	(	)	*	+	,	–	.	/
3	0	1	2	3	4	5	6	7	8	9	:	;	<	=	>	?
4	@	A	B	C	D	E	F	G	H	I	J	K	L	M	N	O
5	P	Q	R	S	T	U	V	W	X	Y	Z	[	\	]	^	_
6	`	a	b	c	d	e	f	g	h	i	j	k	l	m	n	o
7	p	q	r	s	t	u	v	w	x	y	z	{			}	~	DEL

There is a code for capital letters, lowercase letters, and even **punctuation** such as periods and commas. The word "Hi" in hexadecimal is 48 69. "Hi Jethro!" would be written as 48 69 20 4A 65 74 68 72 6F 21.

Top Tip

You'll need to learn that 20 in hexadecimal is a space. Look at row two, column 0.

EVIDENCE BAG CHALLENGE

Scott has found a hexadecimal message on Jethro's computer. It was hidden in a picture of a skateboard deck in the SkateGame Pro chat room. Can you decode the message?

You will need: a pen and paper, the chart on page 24

4d   65 74 20 6D 65 20   74
20   68 65 20 73 6B 61   65
7 0   72 6B 2E 20 44 6F   E
6   20 74 65 6C 6C 20   E
7 6F 6E 65 2E 20 44 4   E

Write a message to a friend using hexadecimal code. Then give your friend the chart so they can work out what the message says.

TRACKING A CELL PHONE

Jethro's parents and Detective Olivier have been trying to contact Jethro on his cell phone. There is never any answer. Scott got the phone number from Jethro's parents. He set to work. Scott has several ways to find where a phone is.

Many modern phones send out **GPS coordinates**. Some phone apps use GPS to tell the user where they are in the world at any time. Scott can organize with the phone's network provider to "ping" a cell phone. When a signal is sent out to the phone, it automatically replies with its GPS location!

Solve It!

Which phone app might use GPS coordinates?

a) a calendar app

b) a clock app

c) a map app

Answers on page 45

EVIDENCE BAG CHALLENGE

Even phones that do not use GPS can still be tracked. A cell phone usually communicates with at least three phone towers at any one time. By comparing the signal strength for each tower, Scott can work out approximately where the phone is.

Can you work out which location Jethro's phone is near, from the information below?

Jethro's phone is 5 miles from tower 1
Jethro's phone is also 3 miles from tower 2
Jethro's phone is also 4 miles from tower 3

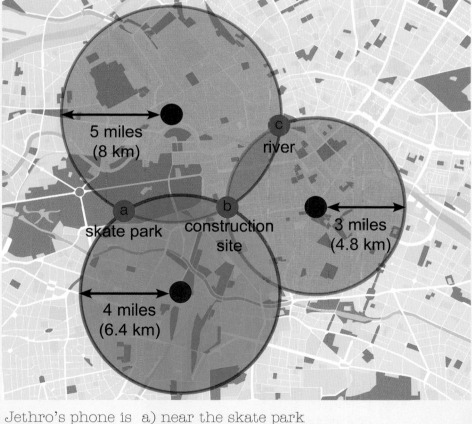

Jethro's phone is a) near the skate park
                   b) near the construction site
                   c) near the river

SCIENCE DETECTIVE

Safety Challenge

The internet is an open space. If you post something publicly, anyone can find it. They can also copy it, save it, and share it. Always be very careful what you put online.

Top Tip

Never post anything online that includes personal information that you wouldn't want a stranger to see.

EVIDENCE BAG CHALLENGE

Have you ever seen how quickly images on social media can get thousands of "likes"? You can use your own social media account to see this for yourself.

You will need: a social media account, a pen and paper, a camera or scanner

 Write a sign similar to this one.

 Post a picture of your sign on a social media account.

Then sit back and wait. You will probably be amazed at how many people see your image in only a few hours.

Remember this whenever you share an image. Once it is shared, you cannot control where it goes.

I am doing a project to see how quickly a picture can be seen by lots of people. Please "like" this picture. Thanks!

☺

Are You Safe?

It is important to keep yourself safe while using the internet. Can you get a high score on this internet safety quiz?

 You shouldn't post any personal information online. What is personal information?
a) your address and phone number
b) your favorite film

 Your friend asks for your password. What do you do?
a) you give it to them, they are your best friend
b) you say sorry, but no

 Someone you met online keeps asking to meet up. What do you do?
a) tell a trusted adult, and don't agree to meet up
b) meet somewhere quiet, so you can get to know each other

 What should you do if you see something online that makes you feel uncomfortable, unsafe, or worried?
a) try not to worry about it
b) leave the website, and tell a trusted adult

 Which of these passwords should you choose?
a) your pet's name
b) a word and number that you'll remember, but no one could guess

 When you are playing a game online, what name should you use?
a) a made-up name
b) your real name

Answers on page 45

TWO BOYS MISSING

Across town, the police are working on another report about another missing boy.

Jay Darsha was looking after his younger brother, Daniel, while their mother was away on business. When Daniel didn't come home on the first night of their mother's trip, his brother wasn't too worried. Daniel is 14 years old, and he often stays at his friend Chris's house and forgets to tell Jay. When Daniel didn't come home the next day, though, his brother got worried. Jay called Chris, who said he hadn't seen Daniel for days. Jay immediately reported Daniel missing. Now the detectives have two boys to find.

Jay tried to check Daniel's computer, to see if anything was written in his calendar that might say where he was. He had no luck. The computer was locked and he needed a password to get in. Detectives ask Scott if he can try to work out what the password might be.

Cracking Passwords

Password cracking is Scott's favorite part of the job. He usually uses computer programs to help him. It can be difficult to get the right answer quickly. Some programs try all the possible letter combinations, one by one, to guess a password. It can be very slow. A password that has seven characters that are all capital or lowercase letters has 8,031,810,176 possible combinations! If a number or symbol is added, or if Scott does not know how long the password is, it will take even longer to crack.

Sometimes, the quickest way of cracking a user password is by guessing. This works best if Scott knows something about the user. People often choose a password that means something to them. Sometimes password-cracking can even be as simple as looking in their desk for a list of passwords!

Can You Guess the Password?

Scott asks Daniel's brother for as much information about him as he can get. Scott wants to know Daniel's hobbies, favorite bands, and the names of any of his pets. These things are often used as passwords.

There are common passwords that people often use, too. Scott usually tries them first. Many people simply type the easiest thing they can. That is why "qwerty" is a very popular password, as it is the first six letters at the top of a keyboard. The passwords "abc123" and "123456" are very common, too. These are not good passwords because they are so easy. Scott tries all these obvious ones, but he doesn't break into Daniel's computer.

Birthplace: Walters Valley

Birthday: March 16th, 2002

Parent's names: Mary and Sam

Brothers and Sisters: Jay, Tanya

Favorite band: The Foo Fighters

Favorite song: Eminem: Lose Yourself

Pets: Mousey the mouse, a German shepherd named Harley

Hobbies: Skateboarding, playing League of Legends, BMX biking

Best friends: Kurt, Polly, and Sebastian

Favorite car: Ford Mustang

Favorite food: Ice cream

Daniel and Harley

Top Tip

One of the most popular passwords of all is "password"! That would be easy to guess!

Solve It!

Scott guesses Daniel's password pretty quickly. Which of these do you think the password might be?

a) Lousey1

b) Housey123

c) Mousey2002

Answers on page 45

keyword searching

Scott and Detective Olivier are beginning to piece together a connection between Jethro and Daniel. Scott now wants to search their computers for anything that links the boys. He starts searching for keywords. Keywords are words and phrases that the boys might have typed that may lead to other useful information. If Scott was investigating a bank robbery, for instance, he might search documents for the name or address of the bank.

Good Keywords and Bad Keywords

It is important to chose good keywords to search with. Some keywords give far too many results.

"Jethro"   This would be a bad keyword. Jethro will have many files and photos which use his name. If his user account is called Jethro, lots of **system files** will pop up in the search, too. There would be too much stuff to search through.

"DD"   Using initials, or very short keywords, is usually a mistake, too. Think how many times the two letters "dd" appear in words. All those words will turn up in your search.

"Walters Valley" This would be a good keyword search as it would not have been used often.

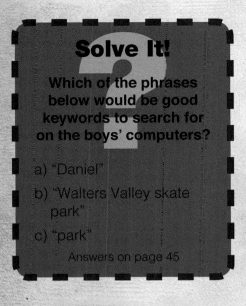

Solve It!

Which of the phrases below would be good keywords to search for on the boys' computers?

a) "Daniel"

b) "Walters Valley skate park"

c) "park"

Answers on page 45

Computer forensics keywords are just like the keywords that you type into an internet search engine. When you search for things, sometimes you get too many results to easily find the thing you wanted among them. Occasionally the keywords bring up too few results. If you misspell a word, you can get a load of wrong results. You must choose your words carefully.

EVIDENCE BAG CHALLENGE

Try this internet search snake game with friends. Compete with friends to create the longest sentence that you can, that still gives you some search results.

You will need: a computer, a child-friendly search engine such as Kidrex, a friend

1. The first player types in one word. For example "The."
   The " " around the sentence means that the search engine looks for that complete sentence, not just some of the words.

2. The next player continues the sentence and types another word. The sentence must make sense. For example "The dog."

3. Each player adds a word in turn until someone gets no results for their search.
   "The dog goes"
   "The dog goes woof woof"
   "The dog goes woof woof bow" got no results, so this player loses.

Homing in on Jethro

Scott searches several keywords on the boys' computers. Chat room messages about the skate park lead him to some more interesting conversations. Jethro and Daniel had talked about doing some street skating after they met at the skate park. Daniel said he knew of a construction site. He thought it looked fun to skate there.

Investigators had already visited the construction site where the cell phone signal was found, but they hadn't found anything. Detective Olivier decides to check again while Scott finishes writing up his report.

Top Tip

When Scott writes his report he has to make sure it can be understood by anyone. He is careful not to use too much technical language.

Halfway through writing up his report, Scott's computer starts to behave oddly. His document freezes and he can't save it. Scott suspects his computer has been infected with a new **computer virus**. He quickly runs some anti-virus software. Sure enough, Scott finds the problem.

The virus may have been hidden in an email attachment he got yesterday from an old coworker. He thought it was odd to get an email from this man, since they hadn't been in touch for years. Viruses are often spread to your computer if you open an infected attachment.

Can you spot the suspicious email in Jethro's inbox?

• From	Subject	Date Received	📎
	Party Invite	Today	📎 1 item
Skatezy.com	sale now on	Today	
	kickflip time!	Today	
lotzprizes.com	You've won!!!!!!!	Yesterday	📎 1 item
	Homework?	Yesterday	
Shoppyshops	Sale time	Yesterday	
	school trip?	Yesterday	
	Phone number	Yesterday	

Answers on page 45

All About Viruses

As a computer forensic scientist, Scott has to investigate criminals who write and spread viruses. A virus can spread rapidly by using your address book to send copies of itself to all your contacts. Some viruses destroy data, too. Viruses cost businesses millions of dollars, as valuable work and time is lost. Why do people create them? Some viruses are written by people with a grudge. Some are created to steal passwords and credit card numbers. Others are created simply to show how poor a computer's security is.

Solve It!

How can you protect your computer against a virus?

a) run special anti-virus software

b) never download free games and software from the internet

c) never open email attachments if you don't know who they are from

d) all of the above

Answers on page 45

EVIDENCE BAG CHALLENGE

Computers follow instructions. If a computer virus makes the instructions go a little wrong it can mess up what the computer is doing. Computer instructions are a little like using a recipe. You have to follow the instructions really closely. If you don't, you might make something pretty weird.

Imagine you are about to cook a meal for your family. You have two lists of ingredients, one for pizza and one for cupcakes. Your recipe file gets a virus, and muddles up the ingredients. Can you see which two instructions in each recipe have swapped, and fix the file before you make a terrible mistake?

Birthday Cupcake Recipe

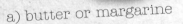

a) butter or margarine
b) granulated sugar
c) 2 free-range eggs
d) vanilla extract
e) fresh basil
f) self-raising flour
g) milk
h) a few drops food coloring
i) decorate with halved cherry tomatoes

Tomato Pizza Recipe

a) salt
b) olive oil
c) bread flour
d) tomato sauce
e) icing sugar
f) garlic clove
g) sliced mozzarella cheese
h) grated Parmesan cheese
i) decorate with candy and birthday candles

LOST BOYS FOUND

Once Scott has sorted out his computer virus problem, he makes a quick call to Detective Olivier. She and her officers are just heading back to the construction site on Park Street to see if there is any sign of the boys. She is hoping to find their cell phones, or something that belonged to them that might give her a clue as to where they went.

It is starting to get dark. When the team enters the site, they hear a faint tapping noise coming from way inside. The team stays silent for a while, trying to work out where the tapping is coming from.

Detective Olivier calls for a police search dog team to come and help. The dogs are trained to sniff out missing people using their sensitive noses.

Solve It!

What do you think might have happened to Jethro and Daniel?

a) the boys were both staying at friends' houses

b) the boys fell and got trapped somewhere at the construction site

c) the boys were kidnapped

Answers on page 45

Top Tip

Computer forensics can help in the search, too. Police sometimes use a device that can mimic a phone control tower. This lets them locate a cell phone's exact location.

never again

The search dog is given an old T-shirt of Jethro's to sniff. He quickly goes to work searching the area. The dog leads the team to a stairwell. The stairs have not been built yet, so the stairwell is actually just a hole, two stories deep. The team now hears the sound of voices. The boys have been found at last!

EVIDENCE BAG CHALLENGE

Dogs' sensitive noses make them ideal to use when searching a building. It is often difficult for people to work out where a sound is coming from. A sound can echo around a space, confusing your brain so it can't work out the direction it is coming from. In this challenge, try to track down a cell phone against the clock!

You will need: a cell phone, another phone, a friend

1. Hide a cell phone somewhere in the house.

2. Call the cell phone's number.

3. Your friend has to find the phone in 10 rings. Can they do it?

4. Take turns hiding the phone. Make sure you remember where you hid it, though, in case the battery dies!

Name: **Jethro Neale**

Missing Person

Missing: 07/21/2017
Found: 07/23/2017

Detective in Charge: Detective Olivier

Jethro Neale was reported missing on the evening of July 21st 2017. Computer forensic scientist Scott Freeman found evidence on Jethro's computer that linked him with missing teenager Daniel Darsha. Chat room conversations suggested that the boys might have gone to a construction site. Freeman tracked Jethro's cell phone to a construction site at Walters Valley. The boys had fallen down a stairwell and suffered minor injuries. After one night in the hospital, both were well enough to return home the following day. They have promised never to skate at a construction site again.

Glossary

accomplice One associated with another in wrongdoing.

chat room An online interactive discussion group on the Internet.

computer forensic scientist A computer specialist who gathers and preserves evidence found in computers and digital storage media.

computer virus A piece of code which is capable of copying itself and usually has a harmful effect, such as corrupting the system or destroying data.

data Information in numerical form for use especially in a computer.

defense The person opposing the claim of another in a lawsuit.

electrons Elementary particles that have a negative electric charge and travel around the nucleus of an atom.

evidence Material presented to a court in a crime case.

GPS coordinates Unique identifiers of a precise geographic location on the earth using a global positioning system.

hard drive A disk drive used to read from and write to a hard disk.

humidity The amount of moisture in the air.

JPEG A format for compressing image files.

profiles A collection of information associated with a user.

punctuation Marks, such as commas, in written matter to make the meaning clear and separate parts.

RAM Random access memory is a form of computer data storage.

static electricity A stationary electric charge, typically produced by friction, which causes sparks or crackling or the attraction of dust or hair.

system files Files that form part of the operating system or other control program.

technician A person employed to look after technical equipment.

transmitters Equipment used to generate and transmit electromagnetic waves.

vibrations The effect of an object moving continuously and rapidly to and fro.

ANSWERS

page 6 - b, page 10 - Meet me at the skate park, page 11 - every fourth word, I will meet you at the corner of 1st Street at 10 p.m., 12 - b, 15 - 1 = blue, 2 = cell phone, 3 = router and computer, 4 = mouse 1, 5 = keyboard, 17 - c, 19 - d, 21 - a, 23 - b, 25 - Meet me at the skate park. Do not tell anyone. DD., 26 - c, 27 - b, 29 - 1 - a, 2 - b, 3 - a, 4 - b, 5 - b, 6 - a, 33 - c, 35 - b, 36 - lotzprizes.com, as it is not from a friend, and has an attachment that might be harmful, 38 - d, 39 - e and i have swapped, 41 - b

Want to be a computer forensic scientist?

Job: Computer Forensic Scientist

Job Description: Computer forensic scientists combine their computer science skills with their forensic skills. Their job is to recover information from computers and storage devices. They help law enforcement officers with any computer-related crimes and help retrieve evidence. They use their technical skills to hunt for files and information that have been hidden, deleted or lost. They must be familiar with all standard computer operating systems, networks and hardware as well as security software and applications. Analysts also must be able to explain the evidence in a way that can be used in criminal trials, and often have to testify in court.

Qualifications needed: A degree in computer science or information technology. Some also have a further certificate in computer forensics. Most computer forensic scientists then learn their advanced techniques on the job.

Employment: Computer forensic scientists usually work for law enforcement agencies, such as the police force.

Further Information
Books

O'Ryan, Ellie. *The Case of the Digital Deception (Club CSI)*. Simon Spotlight, 2013.

Zullo, Allan. *10 True Tales: Crime Scene Investigators (Ten True Tales)*. Scholastic Nonfiction, 2015.

Websites

Follow the experts from the TV show CSI in this game to learn more about how forensic science helps to solve crimes!
http://forensics.rice.edu

Tips for kids and parents on internet safety as well as an interactive educational game, Carnegie Cadets!
http://www.carnegiecyberacademy.com

PUBLISHER'S NOTE TO EDUCATORS AND PARENTS:

Our editors have carefully reviewed these websites to ensure that they are suitable for students. Many websites change frequently, however, and we cannot guarantee that a site's future contents will continue to meet our high standards of quality and educational value. Be advised that students should be closely supervised whenever they access the Internet.

index